Homes around the world

City Homes

Nicola Barber

 Crabtree Publishing Company

www.crabtreebooks.com

Crabtree Publishing Company

www.crabtreebooks.com

Editors: Hayley Leach, Ellen Rodger, Michael Hodge
Senior Design Manager: Rosamund Saunders
Designer: Elaine Wilkinson
Geography consultant: Ruth Jenkins

Photo credits: Arcaid/Alamy p. 15; Bill Bachman/Alamy
p. 21; Michele Falzone/Alamy p. 16; Andrew Holt/Alamy
p. 6; Richard Levine/Alamy p. 20; Mooch Images/Alamy
title page, p. 8; Alex Segre/Alamy p. 23; John
Stark/Alamy p. 24; Ulana Switucha/Alamy p. 19; Janine
Wiedel Photolibrary/Alamy p. 11; Mark E. Gibson/Corbis
cover, p. 7; Robert van der Hilst/Corbis p. 14; Vincent
Laforet/Pool/Reuters/Corbis p. 18; Demetrio
Carrasco/Getty p. 17; Paul Cchesley/Getty p. 10, p. 27;
Wendy Chan/Getty p. 22; Yann Layma/Getty p. 12; Felix
St Clair Renard/Getty p. 9; John Henry Claude
Wilson/Getty p. 25; Jane Sweeney/Lonely Planet Images
p. 13, p. 26.

Cover: Townhouses and skyscrapers
in San Francisco, California.

Title page: Rows of townhouses line the edge of the
River Seine in Paris, France.

Activity & illustrations: Shakespeare Squared
pp. 28, 29.

Library and Archives Canada Cataloguing in Publication

Barber, Nicola
    City homes / Nicola Barber.

(Homes around the world)
Includes index.
ISBN 978-0-7787-3542-7 (bound).--ISBN 978-0-7787-3554-0 (pbk.)

    1. City dwellers--Dwellings--Juvenile literature. 2. Dwellings--
Juvenile literature. I. Title. II. Series: Barber, Nicola. Homes around
the world.

GN395.B37 2007   j392.3'6091732   C2007-904712-2

Library of Congress Cataloging-in-Publication Data

Barber, Nicola.
    City homes / Nicola Barber.
        p. cm. -- (Homes around the world)
    Includes index.
    ISBN-13: 978-0-7787-3542-7 (rlb)
    ISBN-10: 0-7787-3542-7 (rlb)
    ISBN-13: 978-0-7787-3554-0 (pb)
    ISBN-10: 0-7787-3554-0 (pb)
    1. Dwellings--Juvenile literature. 2. City and town life--Juvenile
literature. I. Title. II. Series.

GT172.B35 2008
392.3'6--dc22   2007030180

Crabtree Publishing Company
www.crabtreebooks.com   1-800-387-7650

Published in Canada
Crabtree Publishing
616 Welland Ave.
St. Catharines, Ontario
L2M 5V6

Published in the United States
Crabtree Publishing
PMB16A
350 Fifth Ave., Suite 3308
New York, NY 10118

Published by CRABTREE PUBLISHING COMPANY
Copyright © **2008**

Contents

Words in **bold** can be found in the glossary on page 30

What is a city home?

A city is a place where thousands, sometimes millions, of people live and work. There are many buildings in a city, such as offices, stores, factories, and homes.

▼ About six million people live in the city of Rio de Janeiro, Brazil, in South America.

Cities can be very crowded places. Some people live in large houses. Many people live in tall buildings that contain a lot of homes. These are called **"apartment buildings"**.

◄ *These houses are in San Francisco, California. There are office buildings in the distance.*

City life
The world's tallest building is in the city of Taipei in Taiwan.
It is 1,670 feet (509 meters) high!

Townhouses and suburbs

In some cities, the streets are lined with houses that are all joined together in a long line. These are called **"townhouses"** or **"terraced** houses".

▼ *Rows of townhouses line the edge of the River Seine in Paris, France.*

Many people have their homes outside of the city center in areas called **"suburbs"**. The suburbs are often located many miles from the city center. Despite their distance, they are still part of the city.

▲ *These houses are in the suburbs of Stockholm, the capital city of Sweden.*

Shanty towns

Across the world, people are moving from their homes in villages or the country to live in big cities. It is often easier to find work in a city than it is in the country. People may not have enough money for a home in the city, so they build **shelters** in **shanty towns**.

▼ People in this shanty town have built their homes from wood and **corrugated iron** in Ho Chi Minh City, Vietnam.

Some city people do not have homes. They live on the city streets. They make shelters from bits of cardboard and plastic. There are homeless people in big cities all around the world.

▲ *This woman lives in a shelter on the streets of London, England.*

Building a city home

Many city people live in apartment buildings. These tall towers are made from **steel, concrete,** and glass. Builders use the steel to make a strong **frame** for the building. They use the concrete and glass to make the walls and windows.

▼ *People have no gardens in these apartments in Wuhan, China. Their **balconies** are the only outside spaces.*

In other places, city homes are built using **materials** found nearby, such as mud or stone. People mix the mud with straw to make the building stonger.

▲ *Many of the mud houses in Kano, Nigeria, have decorations on their roofs.*

13

Inside a city home

Many cities are expensive and crowded places to live, and a lot of people cannot afford large homes. Families often live in small apartments. People may live, eat and sleep in just one or two rooms.

▼ *This woman lives in a small apartment in Shanghai, China.*

To find more space to live in, people have **converted** old buildings into homes. Many of these buildings were once **warehouses** or offices. Now they are full of apartments.

▲ *This woman lives in Glasgow, Scotland. Converted apartments often have a lot of space.*

The weather

In very hot places, people try to keep their city homes cool. In some cities, buildings have wind catchers on top. These wind catchers are like wide chimneys facing toward the wind. They trap the wind, and the air goes into the rooms below.

▼ The city of Yazd, Iran, lies in the middle of a hot desert. Wind catchers help cool houses there.

It can get very cold during the winter in some cities. The city of Moscow, Russia, has snow on its streets in winter. Hot water is pumped through pipes to keep homes warm. People turn on electric radiators when the temperature drops very low.

City life

In 2006, the temperature went as low as −36° Fahrenheit (−38° Celsius) in Moscow.

▲ Winter in Moscow is so cold that canals and rivers freeze over.

The environment

A storm or **earthquake** can cause a lot of damage in cities because there many buildings. In 2005, a **hurricane** hit near the city of New Orleans, Louisiana. It caused massive damage and flooding. A hurricane is a big storm with rain and strong winds.

▼ *After a hurricane in New Orleans,* **floodwater** *from the Gulf of Mexico filled streets and homes with water.*

Often, the air in cities is not very clean. Smoke from factories and **exhaust fumes** from **vehicles** make the air dirty. Sometimes, a city is covered with a cloud of air **pollution** called "**smog**".

City life

In 1995, an earthquake in Kobe, Japan, killed more than 6,000 people.

▲ *In this picture, you can see smog lying over the **skyscrapers** of Hong Kong, China.*

School and play

City schools can be very big, with hundreds of students. Some children may have come to the city from other countries. Students at a school may know many different languages.

▼ *These girls are using computers at a school in New York City.*

There are many different things to do in a city. Children can visit parks and city zoos. There are theaters and cinemas for going to see plays and films. There are libraries for reading books. There are swimming pools and places for playing sports.

▲ Actors perform a play outdoors in a park in Melbourne, Australia.

Going to work

City centers often have tall buildings called "skyscrapers", which are full of offices where people work. Other people work in factories to make things, or on the cities' buses and trains.

▼ *Thousands of people work in these skyscrapers in Singapore.*

In city centers, people work in big **department stores**, as well as in small stores. People often come to the city to go shopping. When they are not at work, many people go to the theaters and restaurants in the city.

City life
Macy's in New York City is the largest department store in the world.

▲ Galeries Lafayette is a department store in the center of Paris, France.

Getting around

There are many different ways to travel around a city. Some cities have trains called "subways" that go through tunnels underground. Other cities have **streetcars** that run on rails in the streets.

▼ *People are getting on and off of a subway train in Hamburg, Germany.*

Many people drive cars in cities. City streets are often full of cars. Sometimes, cars stuck in traffic move so slowly that it takes a long time to go even a short distance.

▲ Cars and other vehicles are stuck in a long traffic jam on this street in Kolkata, India.

Where in the world?

Some of the places talked about in this book have been labeled here.

Look at these two pictures carefully.

- How are the homes different from each other?

- What is each home made of?

- Look at their walls, roofs, windows and doors.

- How are these homes different from where you live?

- How are they the same?

NORTH AMERICA

San Francisco

New York

New Orleans

ATLANTIC OCEAN

PACIFIC OCEAN

SOUTH AMERICA

Rio de Jane

Kano, Nigeria

N
W   E
S

EUROPE

ASIA

Stockholm

lasgow

Moscow

Hamburg

ris

FRICA

Dubai

Kano

Wuhan

Kolkata

Kobe

Shanghai

PACIFIC

OCEAN

Hong Kong

Ho Chi Minh City

Singapore

*Ho Chi Minh
City, Vietnam*

AUSTRALASIA

Melbourne

ANTARCTICA

Cityscape mobiles

Create your own cityscape mobile

What you need
- several sheets of paper
- single-hole punch
- scissors
- glue
- pencil crayons or markers
- hanger
- yarn
- pencil

1. What types of buildings do you find in cities? Take another look through this book to help you remember.

2. On a piece of paper, draw a picture of each type of building that you want to include in your cityscape. Color the pictures with pencil crayons or markers.

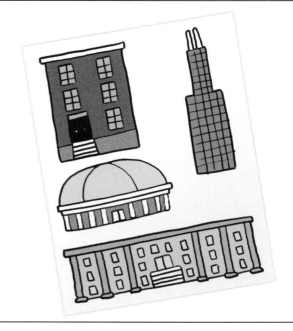

3. Cut out each building. Place each cut-out on a piece of paper, and trace around each one. Draw in details and add color to make each outline look like the buildings that you created in step two. Cut out these buildings.

4. Glue the blank side of each pair of buildings together.

5. Punch a hole at the top of each building. Cut a six-inch piece of yarn for each building. Loop the yarn through each hole, and tie a knot. Tie the other end of the yarn to the hanger.

Big City Living
Answer the following questions.
Share your answers with a classmate.

If you could live in any large city in the world, what city would you choose?

What type of building would you call home?

What type of job would you have in this city?

How would you get from place to place?

What would you do for fun?

Glossary

apartment	A set of rooms to live in, usually on one floor of a building
balcony	A small platform with rails that sticks out of a building
concrete	A mixture of cement, sand and water that is hard when dry
convert	To change into something else
corrugated iron	A sheet of iron that has ridges running along it
department store	A large shop with many different sections
earthquake	When the ground moves and shakes
exhaust fumes	Waste gas that comes from the engine of a vehicle
flood	When water goes onto land that is normally dry
frame	A structure that gives something shape and strength
hurricane	A storm with strong winds and a lot of rain
material	What something is made of
pollution	Something that is dirty and dangerous to people
shanty town	An area of roughly built homes
shelter	Any structure that provides some cover from the weather
skyscraper	A very tall building
smog	Dirty air
steel	A kind of metal that is very strong
streetcar	A kind of train that runs on rails set into the street
suburb	An area of homes on the edge of a city
terraced	Describes houses that are joined together in a long line
townhouse	A house that is joined to its neighbours
vehicle	Any kind of transport with wheels, such as a car or a truck
warehouse	A large building that is used to store goods

Further information

Books to read

Early City Life, from the Early Settler Life series
Early Village Life, from the Early Settler Life series
Life in a Castle, from the Medieval World series
Extreme Structures, from the Science Frontiers series
Green Power, from the Science Frontiers series

Websites

http://www.un.org/cyberschoolbus/habitat/index.asp
United Nations CyberSchoolBus website about cities

http://www.bbc.co.uk/schools/twocities/
Compare Belfast and Mexico City online

http://www.tlcarchive.org/htm/home.htm
Historical information on city life in New York City
and the United States

Index

All of the numbers in **bold** refer to photographs.